CALIFORNIA

Oregon
Nevada
Arizona
MEXICO
PACIFIC
OCEAN
Point St George
Redwood National and State Park
Trinidad Head
Eureka
Cape Mendocino
Point Delgada
Point Arena
Point Reyes
Klamath R.
Clair Engle L.
Shasta L.
Redding
Lassen Volcanic N. P.
Godse Lake
Alturas
Pit R.
Eagle L.
Susanville
Honey L.
Eel R.
Chico
Feather R.
Yuba City
Lake Tahoe
Clear L.
Russian R.
Roseville
SACRAMENTO
Elk Grove
Santa Rosa
Vallejo
Concord
Oakland
San Francisco
Daly City
Hayward
Fremont
Sunnyvale
San Jose
Stockton
Modesto
Merced
Mokelumne R.
Stanislaus R.
Merced R.
Yosemite N. Park
Mono Lake
Kings Canyon National Park
Owens R.
Owens Lake
Death Valley National Park
Fresno
San Joaquin R.
Sequoia N. P.
Visalia
Porterville
Delano
Kern R.
Bakersfield
Buena Vista L.
Monterey Bay
Salinas
Point Pinos
Pinnacles N. P.
Point Sur
Salinas R.
Point Piedras Blancas
Point Buchon
San Luis Obispo
Santa Maria
Point Arguello
Point Conception
Santa Barbara Channel
Channel Islands National Park
Channel Islands
Oxnard
Lancaster
Palmdale
Victorville
Santa Clarita
Glendale
Los Angeles
Fontana
San Bernardino
Riverside
Anaheim
Santa Ana
Long Beach
S. Pedro Channel
Joshua Tree National Park
Palm Springs
Indio
Salton Sea
Colorado River
Oceanside
Escondido
Gulf of Santa Catalina
San Diego
El Cajon
Chula Vista
El Centro
5
80
15
40
10
8

CALIFORNIA

THE GOLDEN STATE

Jacqueline Hope Raynor

Firefly Books

A FIREFLY BOOK

Published by Firefly Books Ltd. 2025

First Printing

Library of Congress Control Number: 2025933807

Library and Archives Canada Cataloguing in Publication
Title: California : the Golden State / Jacqueline Hope Raynor.
Names: Raynor, Jacqueline Hope, author.
Description: Includes index.
Identifiers: Canadiana 20250165694 | ISBN 9780228105657 (hardcover)
Subjects: LCSH: California—Guidebooks. | LCSH: California—Description and travel. | LCGFT: Guidebooks.
Classification: LCC F859.3 .R39 2025 | DDC 917.9404/54—dc23

Published in Canada by
Firefly Books Ltd.
50 Staples Avenue, Unit 1
Richmond Hill, Ontario
L4B 0A7

Published in the United States by
Firefly Books (U.S.) Inc.
P.O. Box 1338, Ellicott Station
Buffalo, New York
14205

Cover and interior design: Jacqueline Hope Raynor
Photo Editor: Cathy Hoshino

Printed in China | DC

FSC www.fsc.org MIX Paper | Supporting responsible forestry FSC® C188448

INTRODUCTION

California's motto, *Eureka*, translates into English as "I have found it." This refers to the discovery of gold in the Sierra Nevada mountain range in 1848, but it also echoes the feelings of those who experience this remarkable state.

California is a state of great contrasts. Its highest point, Mount Whitney, reaches to nearly 15,000 feet above sea level, and its lowest, Death Valley, is 282 feet below sea level. The U.S. has a population of 340 million people, and nearly 10 million of them live in Los Angeles County alone. Yet there are enormous stretches of desert and forest that are barely populated.

This book provides only a sampling of the state's scenic wonders and great cities. Your tour starts in the north with the majestic beauty of Mount Shasta and ends in the south where oases and deserts seem oblivious to the passage of time. Along the way there are detours to some of the state's most historic Spanish missions, where much of California's history began.

Moving south, you will visit world-famous wineries and lush vineyards, then stop at historic Berkeley, home to the founding campus of the University of California. From there you will journey to San Francisco, one of the most beautiful and cosmopolitan cities in the world.

A visit to the High Sierras is next, with its renowned national parks, crystal-clear lakes and snow-capped mountains. A trip down the Pacific Coast offers breathtaking vistas. Moving inland, you will find the arid but beautiful sand dunes of Death Valley and the Mojave Desert.

The next stop is Los Angeles County, with the glamor of Hollywood, followed by a visit to Orange County and the magic of Disneyland. Next on the tour is San Diego County, with scenic coves and a remarkable zoo and, finally, the jaw-dropping magnificence that is Red Rock Canyon State Park.

From the grandeur of its parks to the stark beauty of its deserts, from spectacular coastal scenery to fertile vineyards, and from cosmopolitan cities to lively coastal towns, the state offers an abundance of treasures. We hope you'll enjoy them as you travel through the pages of *California: The Golden State*.

The willowy branches and delicate flowers of almond trees grace a grove in Sacramento Valley. California produces 80 percent of the world's almonds, the state's number one agricultural export.

(Opposite) The California State Capitol building in Sacramento houses the California State Legislature and the Office of the Governor. The design of the building, constructed between 1861 and 1874, is based on the United States Capitol building in Washington D.C. During the Gold Rush, Sacramento was the western terminus for wagon trains, stagecoaches, riverboats, the Pony Express and the transcontinental railroad.

(Previous) Mount Shasta, a potentially active volcano at the southern end of the Cascade Range, stands within the Shasta-Trinity National Forest. It is the largest National Forest in California covering over two million acres. It is managed by the U.S. Forest Service and encompasses five wilderness areas, hundreds of mountain lakes and more than 6,000 miles of streams and rivers.

Castello di Amorosa, a winery located near Calistoga in the Napa Valley, opened to the public in 2007. This authentically styled 14th century Tuscan castle includes 107 rooms on eight levels and covers 121,000 square feet. The complex includes a moat, a drawbridge, defensive towers, an interior courtyard, a torture chamber, a chapel, a knights' chamber, and a great hall with a 22-foot-high coffered ceiling.

(Previous) Bodega Bay in Sonoma County has breathtaking views and beautiful beaches that have been the backdrop for a number of movies, the most famous being Alfred Hitchcock's 1963 classic, *The Birds*. The area is also a bird-watching paradise; the diverse habitats of the bay support a wide variety of species such as the snowy plover, brown pelican and various shorebirds.

Mission San Carlos Borroméo de Carmelo, founded at the present site in 1770, was once the headquarters for the entire California Mission system. It is commonly known as the Carmel Mission, and many consider it to be architecturally the most beautiful of all the California missions.

(Opposite) Point Reyes in Marin County, across the Golden Gate Bridge and about 30 miles outside San Francisco, is said to be the windiest place on the Pacific coast. The Point Reyes Lighthouse, no longer in use, was built in 1870.

The University of California, Berkeley, established in 1868, is the founding campus of the University of California system and currently has an enrollment of more than 45,000 students. Berkeley gained a worldwide reputation for political activism in the 1960s, most conspicuously during the Civil Rights Movement. Berkeley is now widely regarded as a leading center for collaborative mathematical research, drawing thousands of visiting researchers from around the world each year.

(Opposite) Stanford University, founded in 1885, counts 36 Nobel laureates within its community and is consistently one of the top-ranked universities in the world. It has one of the largest campuses in the country, stretching over 8,180 acres.

The Cathedral of Christ the Light, also called Oakland Cathedral, is part of a larger complex that includes a conference center, rectory, health clinic, mausoleum, cafe and shop, public plaza and garden. The first cathedral to be built wholly in the 21st century, one of its design objectives was a reduced ecological footprint; with the exception of evening activities, the cathedral is entirely lit by daylight.

(Opposite) The San Francisco-Oakland Bay Bridge, locally called the Bay Bridge, is a complex of bridges spanning San Francisco Bay. Part of Interstate 80 and the direct route between San Francisco and Oakland, it has one of the longest bridge spans in the United States. It is also the busiest bridge in the state, carrying over 250,000 vehicles a day.

The 210-foot-tall Coit Tower on Telegraph Hill was bequeathed to the city by Lillie Hitchcock Coit, an eccentric philanthropist, with the intent of beautifying the city. The Art Deco tower, completed in 1933 and built of unpainted reinforced concrete, features multiple fresco murals. It was added to the National Register of Historic Places in 2008.

Mission Dolores Park, located at the western edge of the Mission District, is a popular spot for locals and visitors alike. As well as yards of green inviting lawns and an unobstructed view of downtown San Francisco, the park contains tennis courts, a basketball court, a soccer field, a children's playground and a dog park. On a sunny weekend the park is visited by up to 10,000 people a day.

The missions along California's El Camino Real (the Royal Road) represent the first arrival of non-Native Americans to the state. Mission Dolores is the oldest intact building in the City of San Francisco. It opened in 1776 and has witnessed more than two centuries of history, including the 1848 Gold Rush and the earthquake of 1906.

(Opposite) San Francisco's Lombard Street is famous for a steep section with eight sharp turns, which has earned it the distinction of being the "crookedest street in the world." Located along the eastern segment in the Russian Hill neighborhood, it is a major tourist attraction, receiving around two million visitors per year and up to 17,000 per day on busy summer weekends.

Brightly colored Victorian homes are a San Francisco trademark. The tradition of painting houses in rainbow hues began after the Civil War; the buildings are affectionately referred to as "painted ladies." The two tallest buildings in the city can be seen on the skyline: The Salesforce Tower (right) has been San Francisco's tallest building since its construction in 2018; before that, the Transamerica Pyramid (left), erected in 1972, held the title.

(Opposite) The Palace of Fine Arts in San Francisco's Marina District was originally constructed for the 1915 Panama–Pacific International Exposition. Throughout the Bay Area the elegant setting is a favorite location for weddings.

Beloved by tourists and residents alike, cable cars have been a fixture of the city for more than 150 years. At its peak in 2019 the cars made up to 480,000 passenger trips per month. San Francisco's cable cars are one of only two street railways to be named a National Historic Landmark, along with the St. Charles Streetcar Line in New Orleans.

(Opposite) Alcatraz Island, commonly referred to as The Rock, has served as a lighthouse, a military fortification, a military prison and, most infamously, a federal prison. For almost two years (1969-1971), the island was occupied by Native American groups protesting various government policies directed toward the Native population. In 1972, Alcatraz was transferred to the Department of the Interior and became part of the Golden Gate National Recreation Area. Visitors can reach this historic site by a ferry that leaves from Pier 33.

Washington Square Park is an urban oasis in the city's lively North Beach neighborhood. The distinctive Saints Peter and Paul Church sits across from the park, and restaurants and cafes fill the surrounding streets. Over the years, the Square has been a place of refuge for many, notably in 1906 when some 600 people lived in wooden barracks and army tents for a year after the earthquake and fire.

(Opposite) The 16th Avenue Tiled Steps, known locally as the Moraga Steps, is a stairway in the Golden Gate Heights neighborhood. *Fodor's Travel Guide* calls it "possibly the world's largest mosaic staircase." At 90 feet high, the flight contains 163 steps which are covered in over 2,000 unique tiles crafted using some 75,000 glass fragments.

Exchange
SOLVE IT
THINK OUT OF THE BOX
GAMES
THINK
OUT OF THE
BOX
PUZZLES
NFL Shop
EXPLORE THE GOLDEN STATE
DOUGHP
The Crystal Shop
CREPES
SAN FRANCISCO'S WILDER WEST
THE CABLE CAR STORE
SAN FRANCISCO

A colony of California sea lions first appeared on Pier 39 in September 1989 and have become a permanent feature and tourist attraction. The Sea Lion Center is an educational arm of the Aquarium of the Bay; naturalists and education staff interact with visitors and school groups with programs and demonstration activities.

(Opposite) Pier 39 is located at the edge of Fisherman's Wharf and is one of San Francisco's most popular attractions. Street performers, restaurants, shops and a marina are all part of the lively scene. The Wharf is also known for the Cannery Shopping Center, Ghirardelli Square and the San Francisco Maritime National Historic Park.

San Francisco's Chinatown is the oldest Chinatown in North America. Its major thoroughfare is Grant Avenue, packed with colorful stores, popular restaurants and souvenir shops. The Avenue is the location of the annual Chinese Lunar New Year parade, one of the largest Asian events in North America.

KEARNY
NO STOPPING
3PM - 6PM
NO STOPPING
TAXI ZONE

The oldest public Japanese garden in the United States, the Japanese Tea Garden is a popular spot in Golden Gate Park. The landscaped grounds feature beautiful gates, monuments and statues, as well as a teahouse that overlooks a tranquil water garden.

(Opposite) The Golden Gate Bridge connects San Francisco to Marin County and the Redwood Highway. When completed in 1937, it was the world's longest suspension bridge. Although it no longer holds the title, the Golden Gate is an internationally recognized symbol of both the city and the state. The bridge is described in Frommer's Travel Guide as "possibly the most beautiful, certainly the most photographed, bridge in the world."

Apple Park, also known as Apple Campus 2, is the corporate headquarters of Apple Inc., situated in Cupertino. Located on over 64 acres, the four-story circular building has been nicknamed "the spaceship" and houses over 12,000 employees. The central courtyard is a green space that features an artificial pond and has been planted with drought-resistant trees and plants indigenous to the area.

(Opposite) Pink salt ponds at Alviso Marina County Park, gateway to the Don Edwards San Francisco Bay National Wildlife Refuge. The water is pink because of tiny, microscopic organisms that have adapted to live in very salty water. The park features a nine-mile dry season loop trail extending around the former marina.

(Previous) The Winchester Mystery House in San Jose was built by Sarah Winchester, heiress to the Winchester Repeating Arms Company fortune. In 1885 she bought a 45-acre ranch and spent the following 36 years expanding the original eight-room farmhouse into the world's most unusual mansion. When Sarah died in 1922, the house contained 10,000 windows, 2,000 doors, 160 rooms, 52 skylights and 47 stairways. But it is the strange quirks that fascinate most visitors: secret passageways, upside-down columns, staircases to nowhere, sealed-off rooms and doors that open to brick walls. Opened to the public in 1923, it still fascinates people over 100 years later.

These humpback whales are lunge-feeding in Monterey Bay National Marine Sanctuary. The area is one of the largest marine sanctuaries in the United States with 276 miles of shoreline. It is home to hundreds of species of marine mammals, seabirds, fish, sea turtles, marine invertebrates and algae.

(Opposite) 17-Mile Drive, hugging the Pacific coastline, passes famous golf courses, mansions and scenic attractions, including Bird Rock and the Del Monte Forest, which is dominated by the Monterey Cypress tree. The drive serves as the main road through the gated community of Pebble Beach; nonresidents must pay a toll to use the road.

Mammoth Mountain has one of the longest ski seasons in North America, which averages from the start of November to Memorial Day. Mammoth Mountain Canyon Lodge (above) is very popular with extreme snowboarding and skiing enthusiasts and attracts visitors from across southern California.

(Opposite) Emerald Bay State Park contains the only island in Lake Tahoe. As well as being remarkably clear and deep blue, Lake Tahoe's water is said to be nearly 100 percent pure.

(Previous) Yosemite National Park was established in 1890 and people travel from around the world to see its wonders. In this picturesque scene, known as Gates of the Valley or Valley View, El Capitan and Cathedral Rock serve as the gates. Rising 3,000 feet into the air, El Capitan is the world's tallest granite monolith. Plunging 620 feet, Bridalveil Fall is a visitor favorite, reachable year-round from the wheelchair-accessible western trail.

Mono Lake, formed at least 760,000 years ago, covers about 70 square miles. The lake's strange tufa towers are actually limestone spires and knobs that develop when freshwater springs mix with the calcium-rich alkaline water of an inland salt lake.

(Opposite) The General Sherman Tree is one of the largest living trees in the world. It is approximately 2,200 years old and can be seen in the Giant Forest of Sequoia National Park.

Bodie is one of the many ghost towns that boomed for a while and then went bust during the California Gold Rush beginning in 1848. At its peak, 65 saloons lined Main Street, and the town had some 8,000 residents. Murders, shootouts, barroom brawls and stagecoach holdups were regular occurrences. By 1943 only three people lived there, and the town was in steep decline. It was saved from permanent obscurity in 1962 with the creation of Bodie State Historic Park and now receives about 200,000 visitors a year.

The Merced National Wildlife Refuge encompasses over 10,000 acres. The refuge plays host to the largest wintering populations of lesser sandhill cranes and Ross's geese within the Pacific Flyway. Each autumn over 20,000 cranes and 60,000 arctic nesting geese migrate from Alaska and Canada to this important breeding ground. They are joined by thousands of other visiting waterfowl, waterbirds and shorebirds. Coyotes, ground squirrels, desert cottontail rabbits, beavers and long-tailed weasels can also be seen year-round.

Sailing stones, sometimes known as racing rocks, are most famously found at Racetrack Playa in Death Valley National Park; the stones seemingly move without animal intervention. The mystery was solved in 2014 when timelapse video footage revealed the rocks at high wind speeds sliding on thin, melting sheets of ice; the phenomena has been named "ice shove."

(Opposite) Badwater Basin, Death Valley National Park, is a stretch of salt flats at the lowest point in North America – 282 feet below sea level. The pool does have animal and plant life, including pickleweed, aquatic insects and the Badwater snail. Badwater Crater, the lowest place on the planet Mars, is named after the basin due to their similarities.

Zabriskie Point is an iconic Death Valley vista, noted for its erosional landscape. The spectacular views from the Point are some of the most photographed in Death Valley National Park.

The dome-shaped Morro Rock is a dormant volcano that rises off the shore of Morro Bay. A causeway connects it with the shore, making it a tied island. Sometimes called the Gibraltar of the Pacific, it has been designated a bird sanctuary for the peregrine falcon and other species.

The endangered California condor soars over the Big Sur coast and the Pacific. North America's largest land bird, it is important in Native American mythology and one of the world's rarest bird species.

(Opposite) Bixby Bridge in Big Sur is located 13 miles south of Carmel. Before it was completed in 1932, a short return trip between Monterey and Big Sur Valley could take as long as three days. The bridge is one of the most photographed places on the west coast. Big Sur is a rugged 90-mile stretch along one of the most breathtaking coasts in the world.

(Following) The Antelope Valley California Poppy Reserve wildflower bloom occurs from mid-February through May and attracts thousands of visitors every year. Eight miles of trails through the gentle rolling hills, including a paved section for wheelchair access, make the park a wonderful place to hike and explore at any time of the year.

Hearst Castle, known formally as *La Cuesta Encantada* (Spanish for "The Enchanted Hill"), in San Simeon, was built by newspaper tycoon William Randolph Hearst. The over-the-top estate is one of the world's great showplaces, combining various styles that impressed Hearst during his European travels. In its glory days in the 1920s and 1930s, the castle included a twin-towered main building, three sumptuous guesthouses and 127 acres of terraced gardens, fountains and pools.

STARLUX AIRLINES

The Hollywood sign, positioned in the Hollywood Hills above Los Angeles, is an internationally recognized symbol of the American movie business. Its 50-feet-high letters were originally created as an advertisement to promote a new housing development in the area.

(Opposite) The iconic gates of Paramount Pictures recall an earlier era. Paramount is the only major classic studio still located in Hollywood. Tours include a behind-the-scenes look at the daily operations of a major motion picture and television facility.

(Previous) The Los Angeles skyline with Dodger Stadium, home of the Los Angeles Dodgers, in the foreground.

Paramount Pictures
STAGE
4

Rodeo Drive in Beverly Hills features three blocks of the world's most exclusive shopping. Its chic stores and upscale restaurants cater to the very wealthy, the very famous and the very curious.

(Opposite) Beverly Hills City Hall, designed in the Spanish Renaissance style and topped by a blue, green and gold tile dome, has been an area landmark since 1932.

Walt Disney Concert Hall in downtown Los Angeles, designed by Frank Gehry, is home to the Los Angeles Philharmonic orchestra and the Los Angeles Master Chorale. Lillian Disney provided the initial funding as a gift to the people of the city.

(Opposite) TCL Chinese Theatre, previously known as Grauman's Chinese Theatre, on Hollywood Boulevard, has hosted many glitzy movie premieres since it opened in 1927. The concrete blocks in the forecourt bear the signatures, handprints and footprints of many celebrities. The outside of the theater was designed to resemble a giant pagoda.

The Broad is a contemporary art museum located on Grand Avenue in downtown Los Angeles. Named for Eli and Edythe Broad, the philanthropists who financed the construction, it opened its doors in 2015. The Broad is home to over 2,000 works by nearly 200 artists, and houses one of the world's leading collections of postwar and contemporary art.

(Opposite) Since its opening in 1922, the Hollywood Bowl (an amphitheater and public park in the Hollywood Hills) has been a popular live music venue, hosting everyone from Billie Holiday to Yo-Yo Ma, under the iconic silhouette of its concentric-arched band shell.

(Following) Opened in 1994, the Petersen Automotive Museum is one of the world's largest and most diverse automotive museums. It has over 100,000 square feet of exhibit space, with hundreds of cars on display and in the Underground Vault, and chronicles over 100 years of automotive history. After extensive renovations, the museum reopened in 2015, sporting a stunning façade featuring a stainless-steel ribbon assembly made of 100 tons of steel.

Fairfax Av

Wilshire Bl
REMBRANDT & INDIA

Royce Hall, on the campus of the University of California, Los Angeles (UCLA), was completed in 1929. It was modeled after a church in Milan and is famous for both its Romanesque style and its superb architecture.

(Opposite) The Chateau Marmont Hotel on Sunset Boulevard is a reminder of an earlier era, when guests included the likes of Greta Garbo and Errol Flynn. Modeled after a castle in France, the historic landmark has survived numerous earthquakes, along with its share of scandals.

The Korean Bell of Friendship (also known as the Korean Friendship Bell) is a massive bronze bell housed in a stone pavilion in Angel's Gate Park, Los Angeles. The bell was a present from the South Korean government to the United States in 1976 symbolizing the friendship between the two countries and celebrating the United States' bicentennial.

(Opposite) Disneyland Park in Anaheim, the first of the Disney theme parks, opened in 1955 and has been visited by more than half a billion guests. The park has nine themed "lands" and occupies over 100 acres. The statue of Walt Disney and Mickey Mouse stands at the end of Main Street, USA, offering this welcome from Disney: "I think most of all what I want Disneyland to be is a happy place ...Where parents and children can have fun, together."

Founded in 1905 and merged with Los Angeles in 1926, Venice is a vibrant neighborhood known for its picturesque homes built around a series of canals. Venice is also famous for its Boardwalk, skate park and Muscle Beach outdoor gym.

(Opposite) Marina del Rey, a charming coastal community with sailboats, beaches and bike paths, is the largest man-made, small-craft harbor in North America. Today, visitors flock to the area for its year-round sunshine and laid-back, California vibe.

Pasadena's Rose Bowl Stadium was built for the January 1, 1923, annual Rose Bowl football game. The Tournament of Roses Parade (also called Rose Parade) is one of the most famous parades in the world and dates to a late 19th-century festival with horse-drawn carriages.

(Opposite) Louisiana Travel's "Feed Your Soul" float, winner of the Showmanship Award, makes its way down Colorado Boulevard during the 134th annual Tournament of Roses Parade. Every square inch of the exposed surface of a Rose Parade float must be covered with flowers or other natural materials.

(Following) Miraculously spared during the devastating 2025 Palisades Fire, the Malibu Pier is one of the few remaining structures in the area. The historic landmark is in the heart of California's surf culture and surfers from around the world come to Surfrider Beach, known for its three-point break that offers surfers rides of 300 yards or more.

ROSE PARADE
presented by HONDA
OneLegacy
WEST
VISTA R
RANGER
Feed Your Soul.

Cafe

Manhattan Beach in southwestern Los Angeles County is one of the country's most expensive coastal towns. Its 928-foot pier features the Roundhouse Aquarium.

(Opposite) RMS *Queen Mary* is a retired ocean liner that is permanently docked in Long Beach Harbor. No luxury was spared during its years on the high seas. When it was retired, the grand ship steamed to Long Beach, and is now a hotel and tourist attraction, bringing alive the ghosts and legends of the great passenger liner era.

QUEEN MARY
THE QUEEN MARY.
EXPERIENCE THE GRANDEST OCEAN LINER EVER BUILT

The Mormon Battalion Historic Site in Old Town, San Diego, honoring the Mormon soldiers who fought during the Mexican War (1846-48).

(Opposite) Torrey Pines State Natural Reserve in La Jolla, San Diego, covering 2,000 acres, is home to Torrey Pines, the rarest pine tree in North America. The eight miles of trails within the park are popular with hikers and beachgoers. During whale migration it is possible to see several species from the cliffs, including humpback whales and gray whales.

Santa Catalina Island, often simply called Catalina, is a rocky island off the Pacific Coast that can be reached by boat, ferry or helicopter. Cars are restricted, and the island is virtually smog-free. The Catalina Casino (which has never been a casino), houses the world's largest circular ballroom (20,000 square-feet) with a 180-foot-diameter dance floor that can accommodate 3,000 dancers.

(Opposite) Huntington Beach is known as Surf City USA because of its nine and a half mile stretch of sandy beach, mild climate, excellent surfing and beach culture.

The San Diego Zoo is one of the largest and most progressive zoos in the world. Since its creation in the 1920s the zoo has been a pioneer in the concept of open-air, cageless exhibits that recreate a natural habitat for the animals. Dedicated to conservation efforts worldwide, the zoo has helped increase populations of endangered animals, both in captivity and in the wild; an example of this is the work they did to bring the California condor back from the brink of extinction. Housing over 12,000 animals, it is the most visited zoo in the United States and considered one of the best zoos in the world.

The Geisel Library is the main library building of the University of California, San Diego and is named for Audrey and Theodor Seuss Geisel, better known as children's author Dr. Seuss. The library houses the Dr. Seuss Collection, containing approximately 8,500 items covering their lives and books.

(Opposite) The legendary Hotel del Coronado sits on Coronado Island, across the bay from San Diego. Built in 1888, it is the second-largest wooden structure in the United States (after Tillamook Air Museum in Oregon) and is designated a National Historic Landmark. It has hosted presidents, royalty and celebrities, and been featured in numerous books and movies.

(Following) Red Rock Canyon State Park has it all: scenic desert cliffs, buttes, spectacular rock formations, Joshua trees and, at night, diamond-studded skies filled with thousands of stars.

PHOTO CREDITS

ALAMY

Panther Media GmbH: 2; ZW Chen:19; robertharding: 41; imageBROKER.com: 47; Panoramic Images: 56–57; Panoramic Images: 58; Michael DeFreitas North America: 74; UPI: 79; ZUMA Press, Inc.: 82; Zoonar GmbH: 86; NaturaLight: 89; Dennis Frates: 92–93

HARTLEY MILLSON PHOTOGRAPHY

Hartley Millson: 50

iSTOCK

LV_Photography: 9; alan64: 32; Spondylolithesis: 49

SHUTTERSTOCK

Rigucci: 6–7; Iv–olga: 8; Gilberto Mesquita: 10–11; Kit Leong: 12; Christopher Pfeifer: 13; Wildnerdpix: 14; Michael Warwick: 15; Sundry Photography: 16; CravenA: 17; Andrey Bayda: 18; yhelfman: 20; FTiare: 21; Nicholas J Klein: 22; Leonid Andronov: 23; Nicholas J Klein: 24; Vadim 777: 25; Grindstone Media Group: 26; Chris LaBasco: 27; joojoob27: 28; Kit Leong: 29; randy andy: 30; Iv–olga: 31; Michael Warwick: 33; Luciano Mortula – LGM: 34; Tupungato: 35; Dragan Jovanovic: 36–37; NorthSky Films: 38; SnapASkyline: 39; A.N.Foto: 40; Stephen Moehle: 42–43; EQRoy: 44; Chizhevskaya Ekaterina: 45; Martina Birnbaum: 46; Kenzos: 48; Jesse Chun: 51; David Rajter: 52; Manuela Durson: 53; Ivanova Ksenia: 54; Barbara Ash: 55; Panas Wiwatpanachat: 59; Larry Gibson: 60–61; Strikernia: 62; 4kclips: 63; Michael Gordon: 64; 4kclips: 65; 4kclips: 66; Felix Lipov: 67; HannaTor: 68; Kit Leong: 69; Steve Cukrov: 70–71; Michael Gordon: 72; Gerry Matthews: 73; Kirk Wester: 75; Chizhevskaya Ekaterina: 76; TierneyMJ: 77; Ken Wolter: 78; PaulDaniel5010: 80–81; mylovefromjesus: 83; Debbie Ann Powell: 84; Sherry V Smith: 85; John Doukas: 87; Sandy Huffaker: 88; Felix Lipov: 90; Pedal to the Stock: 91; kavram: 96

INDEX

The golden sand dunes of Mesquite Flat are among the most photographed locations in Death Valley National Park.